All Scripture references taken from the KJV of the Holy Bible, unless otherwise indicated.

DON'T TEAR DOWN YOUR OWN HOUSE AND DON'T GET LOCKED OUT

Dr. Marlene Miles

Freshwater Press 2025

Freshwaterpress9@gmail.com

ISBN: 978-1-967860-43-2

Paperback Version

Copyright 2025, Dr. Marlene Miles

All rights reserved. No part of this book may be reproduced, distributed, or transmitted by any means or in any means including photocopying, recording or other electronic or mechanical methods without prior written permission of the publisher except in the case of brief publications or critical reviews.

Table of Contents

Don't Tear Down Your Own House 5

Judgment from God 13

So, What Do You Do? 23

Curse on the Whole House 27

Flying Scroll 33

Repent 36

PRAYER POINTS 39

Locked Out 52

Jesus At the Door 60

Ask For Wholeness 71

Temporal Things 81

Bypass the Devil 88

Increase in Spiritual Vision 93

Who Got You That House? 94

What's In the Kingdom? 97

More Money 102

Gifts of God Are Without Repentance 110

Human Error 115

Ask For the Highest Spiritual Thing 122

Dear Reader 125
Prayerbooks by this author 126
Other books by this author 127

DON'T TEAR DOWN YOUR OWN HOUSE
AND DON'T GET LOCKED OUT

Don't Tear Down Your Own House

A fellow once asked me if I thought he was living a cursed life --- well, he must not have known what the curses were. He built a beautiful house if not a mansion, at least a *mc*Mansion, but he doesn't live in it. He hasn't lived in it for three or more years now. He owns it, he still pays for it and its upkeep, and that upkeep has gotten to be substantial. But he doesn't live in it. Instead, he lives thousands of miles away from it in a well—shack while his mansion sits. Is that under the curse?

Ye shall build houses and not live in them
(Deuteronomy 28:30B)

There are too many ways not to live in your own house, not including investment or rental property. Many people have more than one house, but if you don't live in your own primary home, that is under the curse.

Chances are very high that if you have a primary home and don't live in it because of spiritual reasons, then you don't hold other real estate--, well at least not other real estate that you could move into. The above example of being at a distance from your primary residence is one of the ways. His job has sent him around the world, and his beautiful house sits unused, except by the occasional relative interloper.

What are the judgments for playing around with God and not being a serious Christian, or being a Christian at all? There are judgments, but as bad: when the enemy wants to oppress or attack you and you need protection from God, if you are not in Christ how will you get that protection? You are a sitting duck.

That's what this book is about: once you know what the curses are, then you can know if you are in the Curse column or the Blessing column. Once you find out that you are not in the Blessing column, you may say, that you are a man, undone!

Then said I, Woe *is* me! for I am undone; because I *am* a man of unclean lips, and I dwell in the midst of a people of unclean lips: for mine eyes have seen the King, the LORD of hosts. (Isaiah 6:5)

A family has had six different fires in five different homes over many years --- modern homes, not using a wood burning fireplace. Or a wood stove. These fires were not a kitchen fire, or cooking fires, they were more fluke fire, mysterious fires. They say those who suffer fires it means that that bloodline is not supposed to have a house. At least one of those six fires was arson and another is suspected arson--, both by blood relatives. According to the Word of God in Deuteronomy, it is because of adultery in that house or bloodline, not the act of adultery in that physical house, but the person who owns the house in any way is idolatrous or adulterous and that sin is allowed to dwell in the house.

Adultery is sexual immorality, but it is also idolatry when we re adulterous against God.

Who says?

If a bloodline is not supposed to have a house, then who sold that bloodline out? A Curse came and alit on that house or onto that bloodline. What happened and how did it happen?

We may not know when it happened or how it happened. The house flood, the house loss and devastation, hurricane, tornado. What is happening in that house or that bloodline and houses, in the spirit? It will eventually show up in the natural. or on that land or in that bloodline. What brings forth such? Or allows it? Without cause a curse won't alight.

Adam and Eve were in a *house*, the Garden of Eden, then there was adultery against God, and they got put out. An angel was placed there that had a flaming sword that turned every which way – oh, Fire. Adam and Eve were kept out by Fire. There's that fire. Without sin the curse won't alight.

What can a person do to make sure it doesn't happen to them?

Let's say every house you move into all kinds of strange things happen to it and it needs constant upkeep. Maybe it's even a new and modern house? Spiritual work may need to be done ,prayer, consecration, fasting, observing disciplines of the Faith and obedience to God. Making decrees and declarations over the house. It may not be by any fault of your own, but it could be, but it may not be. It could be because of evil foundation, evil you may have inherited. Evil foundation can cause your house to look a certain way even if you are walking upright before the Lord, but it doesn't look like it.

Destruction of Houses – spiritual – not literal… that should be obvious to all of us. Someone dropped a bomb? Not that, we are talking about spiritual reasons. But when the spiritual has been in place long enough there will be manifestations in the natural realm. When a spiritual deficit or spiritual debt is in place, eventually it will show up in the natural.

Let it be done on Earth as it is in Heaven means that Heaven is our model and we should be trying to emulate and make our world here look like that. If a team was sent to Mars to build a colony, what would they do? Copy what they had on Earth, make it look the same.

In the Garden at Eden God let Adam name all the animals and what he called them, that's what God said their name would be.

Saints of God, what you allow in your life becomes what is allowed in the spirit that involves you. What you allow in the spirit becomes imprinted in the spirit and it will continue into the next generation, unless you or someone with the right authority disallows it.

A man has a house, but he hates mowing the lawn. His lawn looks terrible, uncared for, unkempt. He might even have a car on blocks in the driveway. The whole place looks like impoverished squalor.

That is a statement. That is what that man allows in his life. Disorder. Chaos. Messiness. Go inside his house, if he is the man of that house then inside the house probably looks the same way. His mind might be disordered. Which came first? Don't know, but it is what he allows.

He has a wife and then kids. This man is the man of the house with authority over them – this messiness is what is allowed spiritually, so the *spirits* will not respect you to be anything but a messy, disordered person. By the second or third generation, it is written in that bloodline. It is written in that blueprint. It is written.

Oh, the demons may say, that is a place we can go and romp and play and maybe practice our shenanigans because that place is chaos and that is what we like. That looks like "home" to us.

So, when a man has a certain spiritual order or disorder he is making many statements, what he will accept, what he's not paying any attention to, how he likes his environment, and what he expects to be around him, come to him, or interact with him because of how he has situated or not situated things around him in the natural. All that is a reflection of what is going on the spiritual and what you do or don't do in the natural is spiritual warfare in a sense that the spiritual realm around you will start to look just like your natural realm that you have "named." Like Adam, what you name it is its name.

Judgment from God

> I will smite the winter house with the summer house, (Amos 3:15)

God promises to tear down houses as a sign of judgment for sin (e.g., Amos 3:15 – "I will smite the winter house with the summer house…"). If you are a chronic, unrepentant sinner then expect that your house may be the *payment* for the sin. And because of iniquity if a curse is sent your way, that curse will stick.

Self-inflicted destruction of a house occurs when a person is behaving foolishly or is in sin. Proverbs 14:1 says, "The foolish woman plucketh it down with her hands," meaning a person can destroy their own household through foolish actions, bad stewardship, or strife in the house.

By sin & injustice by being a bad person, such as oppressing the poor or taking bribes can bring ruin to a house (Habakkuk 2:9–10; Proverbs 15:27).

A house can be brought down by neglect or laziness, (Ecclesiastes 10:18). "By much slothfulness the building decayeth; and through idleness of the hands the house droppeth through."

Spiritual tearing down of a house leads to a physical destruction of the house. A divided house cannot stand (Mark 3:25). Division within a household or kingdom leads to collapse. Let there be agreement in your house, not constant bickering. A house divided against itself cannot stand. Let there be agreement and not constant bickering in your house.

Disobedience to God's Word will surely tear up a house. In Matthew 7:26–27, we read, The man who hears God but does not obey is like one building on sand; without a sure foundation the house will fall. When a storm comes, his house will collapse in the storm.

Removing the Cornerstone or the Foundation will bring a structure down. By forgetting God once you get what you want from Him is a sure way to lose that thing. **By ignoring the true foundation, people can destroy their own homes and houses. Folks think that family traditions are the cornerstone of the house or the family; they are not**. Unless the Lord builds the house those that labor, labor in vain. (Christ is the true cornerstone—only Christ. Without a proper foundation and a proper build, what is built will collapse (1 Corinthians 3:11).

Idolatry & false worship, such as setting up idols in the home will tear down a house. God commanded Israel to destroy houses filled with idolatry. By bringing idolatrous things in the house, the house becomes accursed and destruction is imminent. (Deuteronomy 7:25–26; Ezekiel 8:6–18).

We need to know what idolatry is and what is not idolatry. We have to know what idolatry is and what is not. Idolatry is not always bold and, in your face, sometimes it is subtle and hidden. (***This Is Not That*** is a message on my You Tube channel and the book, **This is Not That: *How to Keep Demons From Coming At You***, has much more in it than the message on You Tube.)

For worshiping other *gods*, judgment came on entire households for turning to idols as we see in Joshua 7:24–25. Achan's family was destroyed. Idols are clever – they get worship out of humans in many ways – the latest style, the latest fashion, everyone else is doing this, everyone is going there, everybody else has this---. It will be fun, and no one will know are some of the ways people are coerced into sin. It's just a festival, it doesn't mean anything.

Yes, it does.

No matter how they get worship out of you, even if they trick you, it is still worship.

Bringing cursed objects into the house – "Lest you be accursed like it" (Deuteronomy 7:26). These are things that can bring a house down. Accursed items: items that belong to idols, demons, devils, stolen things, things set aside for God and should not be kept or harbored at your house.

Sin, evil, bloodshed & violence can bring down a house. In the case of murder, blood guilt brings a curse on the murderer's household (2 Samuel 3:29; Proverbs 28:17).

Oppressing the innocent – is not looked upon favorably by God--, like ever.

Woe to him that builds a town with blood (Habakkuk 2:12).

Oppression & Injustice - Defrauding the poor and needy – God promises to tear down the oppressor's house (Proverbs 15:27; Amos 5:11). God would be so clever as to make the oppressor tear down his own house. Think about that when you see awful people, especially those in leadership and government doing awful things. Perhaps God is waiting for their iniquity to be full, but sometimes that person is tearing down their own playhouse.

Perverting justice – Taking Bribes and doing crooked things will bring judgment invite destruction (Isaiah 5:8–9; Micah 2:1–3). Unjust scales, unjust balances-- wickedness.

Stealing land. moving boundary stones will bring a curse. Stealing land brings a curse (Deuteronomy 27:17; Proverbs 22:28).

Immorality & Covenant Breaking with your covenanted spouse and your covenant with God. Will bring judgment on a house. Adultery brings judgment on the household (Job 31:9–12; Proverbs 6:32–33). Breaking covenant with God – The Northern Kingdom's spiritual adultery, which is idolatry led to destruction of homes (Hosea 4:1–3; Amos 3:15).

Using or seeking out sorcery, Witchcraft & Occult Practices. Consulting familiar spirits or magic – Causes God to cut off the soul from His people (Leviticus 20:6; Micah 5:12). Using enchantments or divination in the home – magic. Invites demonic destruction (Deuteronomy 18:10–12). A woman who wouldn't listen and couldn't hear me kept telling me about all the *gifts* in her family how they just *know* things. This was an unsaved family, these were not Gifts of the

Spirit; they were *familiar spirits*, but she didn't know that.

Within a few minutes after she started her tell-all conversation, she also told about the devastating fire they suffered. Python, who is divination, also blocks ears so people can't hear when they should hear. This woman was talking about family "gifts" that were all divination and *familiar spirits*. She didn't realize that this was idolatry. Then came the horrible fire--, where all was lost.

Covenant curses in Deuteronomy 28 starting around verse 15, all the way to the end. When Israel disobeyed, God said Their homes would be seized by enemies (verse 30). Their cities burned (verse 52). Their land and their inheritance taken (verse 63–68). These are ways that a person could not live in a house they own or think they own, even a house they've built.

Summarizing, by bringing in accursed things the house and setting up idols will be set for destruction. By worshipping other gods as in idolatry, the household will be destroyed and possessions burned. By the guilt of murder or bloodshed there will be blood on the family, and the house will be cut off. By oppressing the poor and needy, the house will be torn down by the Lord. This is a reason not to err on the side of stinginess against a poor person. By perverting justice such as in showing favoritism, taking bribes that will lead to the ruin of the house and or the loss of land.

It doesn't mean that all these judgments will happen right away, nor does it mean that it will even happen in the lifetime of the offender. These judgments could be set up for the next generation or the one after that.

Stealing anything, but especially land, even as sneakily as moving boundaries, will bring a curse on the house of the thief. Jezebel and Ahab stole Naboth's land and look at what happened to them.

Pride comes before destruction and haughtiness before a fall. God will destroy the house of the prideful. Make your boast in the Lord. Bragging on how tough or how secure you are, if it is not in the Lord that braggart is setting himself up for destruction. Careful of being house-proud.

Pride comes before destruction and haughtiness before a fall. (Proverbs , James)

Expect the Lord watch the house, those that watch watch in vain.

Adultery brings fire and many other curses. For more on this, recommended: **By Means of a Whorish Father**, book by this author. https://a.co/d/7UEB7te

Idolatry is adultery toward God. Breaking covenant with God got cities burned and houses destroyed. Sorcery, witchcraft and occult practices will cause that diviner to be cut off from God and destruction follows after that.

This includes words, oaths, vows, pledges, declarations and decrees from a blind witch.

Whatever do I mean?

Corruption, in general, whether corrupt politicians, kings, preachers or priests leads to destruction. Anyone who turns a whole nation from God will see destruction. Neglecting and disobeying the commandments of God is where we see that a person may build a house but not live in it. It could be that their enemies take it from him or by some other means. We have said that there are too many ways that a person doesn't live in their own house.

    Laziness, slothfulness, and neglect will obviously bring decay to a house and eventually it will collapse. Sin, disobedience tears a house down.

So, What Do You Do?

If you have or find idols in your house, remove them. Your kids might be the culprits trying to be cool, but not knowing what they are doing. So, remove the items and dedicate or re-dedicate your house to God. Teach your children at all times.

If you or anyone in your house has been worshiping idols or false gods, repent of the behavior and renounce it and worship the LORD God, alone.

If there had been murder or bloodshed in your house or family, aside from the civil criminal issues it brings, repent. Renounce. Denounce. Confess your sins to the Lord and remember to keep the commandments of

God. Thou shalt not kill. Killing is more than physical murder. It could be soul murder. Joseph's brothers tried to kill his dream. If you are guilty of trying to kill or erase someone's ministry, purpose or destiny, that is also murder. Repent and if possible and if the Lord agrees, make restitution.

If you are guilty of mocking or making fun of the poor or the oppressed, repent. Instead of oppressing the poor, defend the poor. Renounce the behavior and then become tenderhearted, kindhearted. Eyelid test… Become a compassionate person full of Mercy. However, if Mercy is naturally your gift be sure it is balanced by the Holy Spirit. Mercy belongs to God so get your permission from God before extending Mercy where it should be given.

If you have taken bribes and perverted justice, repent, of course, and then walk in truth with balance. God hates a false balance. Begin to judge righteously by the Counsels of God. Who does God listen to before making a decision? Avail yourself to the Holy Spirit of God and the seven spirits around the Throne of God.

For laziness and slothfulness – eve complacence, get up and do what you should be doing.

Land thief? Repent. Respect other people's property and property lines. Do not steal, especially do not steal the inheritance of another.

Learn to humble yourself under the Mighty Hand of God if you are one full of pride. Fasting is a great tool to promote humility. Study to be quiet, in many words there is much sin, pride being one of them. Being delivered from narcissism…

Make your boast in the Lord, only.

For adultery, you may need deliverance. That is not often a decision of the mind. For those who say, "What was I thinking?" usually you weren't thinking, a demon was doing the thinking for you and led you into that trap. Adultery is especially bad because the wounded spouse has too much authority to curse the offender.

For slothfulness, get up and get busy. For leading or misleading a nation astray there needs to be immediate and sincere repentance. Covenants of disobedience need to be broken. Broken covenants with God need to be re-instated. National repentance may be indicated. Instead of corrupt leadership, lead with integrity and with the fear of the Lord. The nation rejoices when righteousness rules a nation.

Curse on the Whole House

Zechariah 5:3–4

Then said he unto me, This is the curse that goeth forth over the face of the whole earth: for every one that stealeth shall be cut off as on this side according to it; and every one that sweareth shall be cut off as on that side according to it. I will bring it forth, saith the LORD of hosts, and it shall enter into the house of the thief, and into the house of him that sweareth falsely by my name; and it shall remain in the midst of his house, and shall consume it with the timber thereof and the stones thereof. (KJV)

The curse is active. It is not just a pronouncement, but something God says He will *send forth*. It targets specific sins:

This is an active curse from God.

Stealing (taking what is not yours — could be money, goods, property, land). False oaths (swearing falsely by God's name — breaking covenant, lying under oath, misusing God's name). Blaspheming the name of God.

It enters the house — implying that a curse can reside in a physical dwelling or family line. It remains there until all that it was sent to accomplish is accomplished. It is not a quick strike; it "lodges" in the home. In lodges in that bloodline. Destroys from the inside out. It consumes the *timber and stones*, meaning total structural ruin, not just on the surface.

This is how sin destroys a house. When the curse moves in: how sin destroys a house from the inside out. This is the curse that goes forth over the face of the whole earth. God isn't describing a vague bad feeling. This curse **travels**. It moves with intention, sent out like a law enforcement warrant.

It targets every thief" and "everyone who swears falsely by My name. It doesn't just hang outside, it comes inside. Judgements from God have a **global reach; it can find it's target anywhere. It goes,** over the face of the whole earth.

It crosses the threshold *"...it shall enter into the house..."* The curse isn't content to hover over the offender's head — it **comes inside**. It takes up residence. It affects more than the sinner; it taints the whole household atmosphere. Sin is rarely a private tenant — it invites destructive company.

It settles in and *"it shall remain in the midst of his house."* it doesn't leave. It **stays**. Remains until its assignment is complete. Or there is repentance, and God rescinds the curse or recalls that curse, consuming from the inside out. It will take repentance and seeking the face of God for Mercy to stop it.

It consumes from the inside out *"...and shall consume it with the timber thereof and the stones thereof."* God is making the point: nothing escapes — not the wood, not the stone, not the structure, nor the foundation. This is total ruin — moral, spiritual, physical. None of us want to be in that place with God. You don't just replace a wall; you have to rebuild from scratch.

It consumes from the inside out, Symbolic of long-term spiritual consequences when sin is unrepented.

Therefore, shall my Word... that goeth forth out of my mouth it shall perform that to which I send it.... It will not return void.

If you know you haven't done anything to deserve what you are going through. This is now: how many of your ancestors have done any or all of these things and never repented? Were they even saved? This is why we repent for them now, not to try to get them into heaven, it is so that their iniquity doesn't find us and pollute our foundations. So, we can live and possess the things that pertain to our peace.

This could be why people don't have or keep houses – or get a house or can't stay in a house or their house is or becomes too expensive. These reasons could be why home ownership can be such a stressful struggle. This is why we repent for our ancestors--, not to get them into Heaven if they've already gone on to Glory. It is repentance and asking God to remove the iniquity so we don't keep paying for the sins of the ancestors.

We give respect where respect is due, but the iniquity that ancestors may have created – and we all have sinned and fallen short of the glory of God. The iniquity that our ancestors created lives on, it doesn't magically get erased when that ancestor goes on to Glory. We ask God to forgive and removed that iniquity so we can live and possess the things that pertain to our peace.

And, the ancestor is gone on to whatever other realm that they are due to be in. The ancestor is not an invisible spirit helping you through life. That would be a *familiar spirit;* don't get it mixed up.

1. Lord, in the Name of Jesus any ancestor, relative, household witch, even any evil stranger that has traded my possessions and blessings prophetically before I was even thought of or born to get what they want, sacrificing the future generations of my bloodline –including me. Lord, undo

that sacrifice, undo that deal, undo the curse on my prosperity and let me live, in the Name of Jesus. Amen.

2. Lord, in the Name of Jesus, any relative, household witch, even any evil stranger that has traded my possessions and blessings at any time in my life, Father, undo that sacrifice, undo that deal, undo that curse on my prosperity and life, and let me live, in the Name of Jesus. Amen.

Repent for yourself, in case you did something that you didn't realize was a sin, and repent for the ancestors.

Flying Scroll

God has many weapons of warfare, but in the Book of Zechariah when we talk of Horns and Divine Carpenters, there is a Flying Scroll that is sent out, from the Lord, and that scroll will destroy. (More on this in my book, **<u>Here Come the Horns: Skilled to Destroy.</u>** It is about the horns, but it is also about the Flying Scroll of the Lord.

The Flying Scroll is a weapon of spiritual warfare and those who have the authority to do so may invoke it in battle against the enemies of God. Remember this, however, a two-edged sword cuts both ways.

The following is a very short excerpt from that book's chapter entitled: ***Divine Scroll of God.***

In Zechariah 1:7-6:8, the prophet Zechariah receives multiple visions; eight in total. They are listed with a brief description. We will discuss each in more details later in this chapter as well as have prayers related to the visions and our own deliverance which we seek from the Lord.

- The horseman among the myrtle trees (Zechariah 1:7-17)
- The four horns and four craftsmen (Zechariah 1:18-21).
- The surveyor (Zechariah 2:1-13).
- The vision of Joshua the high priest (Zechariah 3:1-10).
- The golden lampstand and two olive trees (Zechariah 4:1-14).
- The flying scroll (Zechariah 5:1-4).
- The woman in the basket (Zechariah 5:5-11).
- The four chariots (Zechariah 6:1-8).

....

Six: The flying scroll (5:1-4): Zechariah sees a large scroll, written on both sides, flying over the whole land. This vision speaks of God's judgment upon those who disobeyed His law.

"Again I lifted up my eyes and saw before me a flying scroll. 'What do you see?' asked the angel who was speaking with me. 'I see a flying scroll,' I replied, 'twenty cubits long and ten cubits wide.'" (Zechariah 5:1-2)

1. Lord, as with the scroll that the Prophet Zechariah saw, let Your divine law be the judge against the enemies of my soul. Let every horn up against me be judged by Your righteousness, in the Name of Jesus.
2. Lord, as Jesus took captivity captive, make a public show of defeating the horns that have arisen against me and let me be shown to be righteous according to the Blood of Jesus. Let me be vindicated. Let me be restored, back to my first estate or even better, in the Name of Jesus
3. Lord, as You judged the Chaldeans and the Amorites when their iniquity was full, let this be a full Judgment against the horns that have arisen up against Your child, in Jesus' Name.

Father, let Your judgment be swift and unavoidable against the *horns* that have arisen against me, in the Name of Jesus.

Repent

On an airplane flight, if there is turbulence or a loss of cabin pressure, put on your own oxygen mask first. Then help your neighbor.

Sin and iniquity is spiritual turbulence, it is a loss of cabin pressure, therefore, repent for yourself first, then the ancestors. Logically and spiritually, if you're full of sin, how do you expect your prayers for others to be heard? Repent yourself for yourself. Even if you have a friend that you call who helps you sort out things or who prays for you, repent for yourself first. Many times, this will solve the problem. You and God just talk to Him and let him know that you are sorry and that you are turning from your own wicked ways.

It is good that men always repent.

The Way Out: repentance. If sin invites the curse, repentance invites the blessings instead of curses. The opposite of theft is honesty and restitution (Luke 19:8–9). The opposite of false oaths is truth and faithfulness (Psalm 15:1–2). When righteousness moves in, the curse moves out. The curse must go. When light comes the darkness must go. When the blessing comes, the Curse must go. When the blessings come the curse must go. When righteousness comes in, the curse must go.

Instead of stealing we deal honestly with others. Instead of lying and dealing falsely with people we will become generous and deal honestly.

Do not let sin dwell in your house. Purge all evil from your home and dedicate or rededicate it to God. We will invite God in. Ask for the purging, healing Fire of the Holy Spirit so you don't get a destroying fire of the enemy.

3. Lord, consume by Fire the sin, and its effects – not the house, but consume the sin and the iniquity, in the Name of Jesus.

A house built by the Lord with Jesus as the Cornerstone, that house secured by truth and righteousness, a house where the Lord is our defense will stand — not just for this generation, but for the ones to come (Proverbs 12:7). The Lord is our defense and that house will stand. It will be for our peace and our use and our generation and for generations to come. His tabernacle is with men.

By having a house, a man is making a declaration that on Earth, this is how it will be for me. This is how it will be for my family, my children, my *children's* children. Whether with words or not, we do warfare all day long. So, by that man's actions he says that not having a house is not acceptable, but having a house is expected and it shall be. By having a house and securing that house that man is writing in the spirit, **This is how it shall be for my house.** This man is "naming" the things for his life and his family.

As for me and my house, we shall serve the Lord. (Joel 2:28)

You can say the above verse, but if you don't do it or live it, then what have you done?

PRAYER POINTS

4. Lord, Disconnect my house, my name, my address from the grave, in the Name of Jesus.
5. Disconnect my house, my name, my address from death, that my home doesn't die that it is not tied to any evil curse in the Name of Jesus.
6. Lord, silence the violence voices of those enchanting anything evil, in any place against me, mine, or my home, in the Name of Jesus.
7. Lord, disconnect my prosperity and physical strength any wicked power and any evil agent they use, in the Name of Jesus.
8. Lord, give me the ability to buy, own, and maintain my home from all thieves, emptiers, and destroyers, devourers in the Name of Jesus.
9. I repent of, renounce, and denounce all Idolatry -worshipping other gods, in the Name of Jesus.

10. Lord, by Your Spirit, show me all Accursed items in my home and show me how to get rid of them properly, in the Name of Jesus.
11. Lord, let the thunder hammer of God destroy every evil altar in or on this property, in the Name of Jesus. I AM IN CHRIST. I serve the Lord God only, in the Name of Jesus.
12. Lord, I repent for all Murder, all bloodshed, all evil sacrifices ever done in this house or on this land. I denounce all witchcraft and all occultic practices and renounce all initiations and memberships to any evil company, council, coven, or organization whether joined knowingly or unknowingly, in the Name of Jesus.
13. Lord, I sincerely repent of oppressing the innocent, any children showing favoritism-- which is witchcraft and treating them unfairly in the Name of Jesus.
14. Lord, forgive me of mistreating my spouse, in the name of Jesus.

Husbands this is important: Do not mistreat your wife... ever. I will treat her as Christ treats the Church in the Name of Jesus. Else how you treat her will come back on your head.

15. Lord, I repent of Cheating – defrauding the poor, the needy, oppressing the oppressed—Lord I repent for and ask forgiveness for any type of family abuse including elder abuse, in the Name of Jesus.
16. Lord, I repent and ask forgiveness for stealing, in the Name of Jesus.
17. Lord, I repent and ask for forgiveness for adultery, in the Name of Jesus.
18. Lord, I repent for and ask forgiveness for Sin – that I amy have committed knowingly letting sin dwell in the house, in the Name of Jesus.
19. Lord, forgive me for backbiting and backsliding, for sowing or allowing discord in this house, in the Name of Jesus.
20. Father, forgive me for prayerless, carelessness, dry Christianity and breaking relationship with You, in the Name of Jesus.

21. Let me return to You, Lord and please return to me, in the Name of Jesus.
22. I renounce and denounce all Sorcery, witchcraft, occult practices – honoring evil holidays – such as Halloween and any activities that honor idols and devils and little g *gods*, in the Name of Jesus.
23. Lord, forgive me of slothfulness, laziness and neglect. Give me more get up and go in my get up and go, in the Name of Jesus.
24. Amen.

.**Now repent for your ancestors.**

25. I break, dismantle any evil covenants they made that sold you out, sold out your possessions, things that pertain to your peace, and even sold you out for generations in the Name of Jesus.
26. I burn those evil covenants made by evil ancestors, or unsuspecting ignorant ancestors with Holy Ghost Fire – I am in Christ. I blot out the evil signature that bound my bloodline to any curse, in the Name of Jesus.

27. Lord, forgive the sin and iniquity of my ancestors and forget and forgive all iniquity to me and my generations because of their sin, in the Name of Jesus.

If you have a house, have you dedicated it to the Lord God? Then do that. If you have a house and you are not sure how you got it or if it was handed down your family line and you are not sure how they got it – then rededicate that house.

You don't have to call your pastor over or wait until they get a break in their schedule: **You Do It.**

Not only that, denounce serving any false god who may have had or may have taken credit for providing that house to you—and now believe you owe them – but you are in Christ now and will not worship them, so they may be coming at you. dedicate that house, dedicate the land that the house sits on.

The earth was made to help you; speak to the earth that your house sits on.

28. Bow down thine ear to me, deliver me speedily, be thou mine strong rock, Lord be a house of defense to save me, in the Name of Jesus. (Psalm 31:2)
29. Father, in the Name of Jesus, let Goodness and Mercy follow me and let me dwell in the House of the Lord, forever, amen.
30. As for me and my house: we will serve the LORD.
31. I dedicate this house to the Lord and to no other *gods*, in the Name of Jesus.
32. In the Name of Jesus, I apply the Blood of Jesus over this house. Amen.
33. I decree that my house shall not be pulled down by evil covenant, curse or contrary wind, in the Name of Jesus.
34. Holy Spirit do not let my house become desolate, in the Name of Jesus.
35. Through Wisdom a house is built and by understanding, it is established. (Proverbs 24:3)
36. Every effect of cursed house be removed from my house now, in the Name of Jesus.

37. Every effect of cursed land be removed from the land where my house sits, in the Name of Jesus.
38. Lord, be my fortress and strong defense so that no evil can enter this house, in the Name of Jesus.
39. Amen.
40. I seal these words, decrees, declarations and prayers across every dimension, age, era, epoch, timeline, past, present, and future, to infinity. I seal them with the Blood of Jesus and the Holy Spirit of Promise, in the Name of Jesus.
41. Any retaliation against the author, reader, or anyone praying or will ever pray these prayers, decrees and declarations in the future – Lord let that retaliation be rendered null and void and return with Fire on the head of the perpetrator, without Mercy and to infinity, in the Name of Jesus.

So, houses can be destroyed by literal destruction. In the Bible violent raids and warfare were common culprits. Enemies invaded cities and burned down houses. For example, Babylonians destroyed Jerusalem – Jeremiah 39:8; 2 Kings 25:9).

Houses can be lost by falling under Judgment from God. God promises to tear down houses as a sign of judgment for sin as in Amos 3:15 – "I will smite the winter house with the summer house."

By the acts of other men, houses can be lost. Jacob's older boys became enraged and sought revenge. Simeon and Levi destroyed Shechem after the defilement of Dinah (Genesis 34:25–29), taking property and destroying homes.

By siege and fire, in the Bible enemies burn and demolish houses during a siege (e.g., Jeremiah 52:13). Obviously, there are many ways fire can come to a home, this is just one of the ways. Arson is unfortunately still active today. There are upward of 350,000 fires in the USA every year. Sadly about 2500 people die in those fires. Of those 350,000 fires more than 10% of the fires are arson. Up to 40,000 USA fires a year are set.

And worse, the primary subject of this book is when a person tears down their own house as in self-inflicted destruction through foolishness or sin.

Wisdom builds a house, but Proverbs 14:1 – "The foolish woman plucketh it down with her hands," meaning a person can destroy their own household through foolish actions, bad stewardship, or strife. Because of anger, the family who had endured six different house fires, one being set by an angry family member who just burned the house down, confessed to the police and went to jail.

By sin & injustice such as oppressing the poor or taking bribes can bring ruin to a house (Habakkuk 2:9–10; Proverbs 15:27).

By neglect or laziness – "By much slothfulness the building decayeth; and through idleness of the hands the house droppeth through. A man fell through his living room floor into his basement; he did not survive. Accidents happen, but being able to maintain and afford to maintain a house is part of being able to afford the house. Maintaining one's house should not kill a person.

Metaphorically, a house can be torn down. A divided house cannot stand. Mark 3:25 teaches us that division within a household or kingdom leads to collapse.

Disobedience to God's Word as in Matthew 7:26–27 – The man who hears but does not obey is like one building on sand; his house falls in the storm.

Removing the Cornerstone or destroying the foundation or ignoring the true foundation, who is Christ results in collapse (1 Corinthians 3:11).

Samson pulled down a house; he pulled down the Philistine Temple. Though not a "house" in the family sense, Samson's act literally pulled down the pillars and destroyed a building full of people *(Judges 16:29–30)*.

Leprosy Contamination In Old Testament law, if a house had persistent leprosy (mold/mildew), it was torn down (Leviticus 14:45). In our times, certain houses with infestations of certain kinds are burned down or torn down.

Idolatry & false worship, such as setting up idols in the home. God commanded Israel to destroy houses filled with idolatry (Deuteronomy 7:25–26; Ezekiel 8:6–18). Worshiping other *gods* brings judgment came on entire households for turning to idols (Joshua 7:24–25), Achan's family was destroyed for this reason.

Bringing cursed objects into the house – "Lest you be accursed like it" (Deuteronomy 7:26).

Bloodshed & Violence - Murder – Blood guilt brings a curse on the murderer's household (2 Samuel 3:29; Proverbs 28:17). Oppressing the innocent – "Woe to him that builds a town with blood" (Habakkuk 2:12).

Oppression & Injustice Defrauding the poor and needy – God promises to tear down the oppressor's house (Proverbs 15:27; Amos 5:11). Perverting justice – Bribes and crooked judgment invite destruction (Isaiah 5:8–9; Micah 2:1–3).

Pride & Self-Exaltation Trusting in wealth and strength – Nebuchadnezzar's pride led to judgment (Daniel 4:30–31). Boasting in you security apart from God – "The LORD will tear down the house of the proud" (Proverbs 15:25).

Immorality and covenant breaking as in adultery, brings judgment on the household (Job 31:9–12; Proverbs 6:32–33). A Biblical example of breaking covenant with God is when the Northern Kingdom's spiritual adultery led to destruction of homes (Hosea 4:1–3; Amos 3:15).

Sorcery, witchcraft & occult practices consulting *familiar spirits* or magic causes God to cut off the soul from His people (Leviticus 20:6; Micah 5:12). Using enchantments or divination in the home – Invites demonic destruction (Deuteronomy 18:10–12).

Covenant unfaithfulness in leadership as in corrupt kings or priests means that eventually, God tears down their dynasty and dwelling (1 Kings 21:21–24, Ahab; 1 Samuel 3:12–14, Eli). Turning a nation from God – Whole cities and houses burned (2 Chronicles 36:19).

When Israel disobeyed, God listed the covenant curses in Deuteronomy 28. He said that their homes would be seized by enemies (verse 30). Their cities burned (verse 52). Their land and inheritance taken (verses 63–68).

Locked Out

Locked out of being a homeowner, a home buyer can be disheartening, disappointing, or even depressing. Of course, a lot of young people today say they don't want to own a home—they don't want to own anything, they say. They say they don't want any bills, and they never want to get any mail.

Well?

But for those who see the value and purpose in home ownership, being unable to acquire, live in, or keep and enjoy a home is under the curse of the law. As stated, there are many ways a person can own a home and not live in it. By the same token, there are many ways a person can be locked out of ever having a home, in the natural.

We will discuss further some of the ways in the spirit why a person may not be able to buy, have, live in, or enjoy a house or home.

Here are several common factors that can keep a person from buying a home:

Financial Barriers that may complicate or completely block the purchase of a house will follow.

- Low credit score – Makes it difficult to qualify for a mortgage or results in higher interest rates.

- High debt-to-income ratio – Too much existing debt (student loans, car loans, credit cards, etc.) can disqualify buyers.

- Insufficient savings – Lack of funds for a down payment, closing costs, or moving expenses.

- Unstable income or employment – Lenders prefer steady, verifiable income; inconsistent earnings may block approval.

Market & Economic Conditions

- High home prices – In some markets, prices simply exceed what buyers can reasonably afford.

- High interest rates – Makes monthly mortgage payments significantly higher.

- Inflation and rising costs – Eats into disposable income, making saving and affording a mortgage harder.

- Low housing inventory – Fewer homes available drives up competition and prices.

Personal Circumstances

- Job instability or relocation risk – Someone who expects to move soon may not commit to buying.

- Poor financial habits – Overspending, lack of budgeting, or failure to manage credit responsibly.

- Life stage or uncertainty – Some delay buying due to waiting for marriage, children, or retirement planning.

Practical & Legal Barriers

- Ineligibility for financing – Not qualifying for government-backed loans (FHA, VA, USDA) or conventional loans.

- Past financial issues – Bankruptcy, foreclosure, or delinquent accounts on record.

- Unfavorable appraisal or inspection – A home may not appraise at the sale price, or needed repairs make financing impossible.

- Legal/immigration status – Certain visa holders or undocumented residents may face restrictions with lenders.

- Redlining

- Prejudicial lending or denials

   The point of this list is not to make anyone feel bad, it is to show in the natural what would or could delay or block being able to attain a home. Now, look deeper. Of all those things, there is something in the spiritual realm that started or remains or promotes each or any of those situations. When you see the pattern forming from it's inception – and of course it is the devil or his agents, that is the time to begin to act spiritually and also in the natural to make sure the devil's chess move is not successful against you.

For example, if you see that job stability is beginning to be a problem, the problem isn't just job instability, it is all the things that job instability can create. Each thing that doesn't go right in a person's life the big picture needs to be assessed and handled. Start in the spirit. Start with prayer and your Christian walk. Ask God to help you work out the problems that you see arising in your life. Do it as early as possible.

Several reasons why a person might not be able to get or rent an apartment:

Financial Reasons may include any of the following:

- **Low or unstable income** – Landlords often require proof that tenants earn 2–3 times the monthly rent.

- **Bad credit history** – Missed payments, collections, or bankruptcy can be red flags for landlords.

- **High debt load** – Too many obligations compared to income can signal risk.

- **Insufficient funds for deposit and fees** – Upfront costs (security deposit, first month's rent, application fees) can block approval.

Rental history issues such as past evictions can be a major deterrent for many landlords. As well, negative landlord references – Reports of late rent, property damage, or conflict. Or, short or inconsistent rental history – Makes a tenant seem less reliable.

Background Check Problems

- **Criminal record** – Some landlords (or local laws) restrict renting to those with certain convictions.

- **Fraud concerns** – Falsified pay stubs, fake references, or inconsistent application details.

Practical & Market Barriers

- **Tight rental market** – High demand and low supply can push applicants out.

- **Discrimination** – Though illegal, some renters still face bias (e.g., race, family status, source of income).

- **Pets** – Restrictions or extra fees may exclude renters with animals.

- **Large household size** – Too many occupants for the unit or lease terms.

Other Circumstances may include:

- **Lack of rental documentation** – Missing ID, proof of income, or references.

- **Unstable employment** – Frequent job changes or temporary work raises landlord concerns.

- **Unmet requirements** – Some places require renters insurance, cosigners, or guarantors that the applicant can't provide.

In short: money, history, background, and market conditions are the biggest hurdles. But, as a wise Christian with spiritual insight or vision, you may look in your foundation and find things that need to be sorted out at the source so the factors that lead to home ownership, or home security will not be adversely affected in your life.

Jesus At the Door

Jesus stands at the door and knocks.

Why is Jesus standing at the door of your house? I can understand some of your friends, fake friends, ex's, relatives, or in-laws, but surely, not Jesus. Why haven't you let Jesus in?

Who got you the house? What God were you serving when you got the house? Were you serving Jehovah, or some other *god*? We need a house to function properly and safely in this life. Where did you get the gift? Whoever you got the gift from is who holds the mortgage – the power to let you in, dwell in peace or to push you out or keep you out.

Adam & Eve, Garden of Eden; they had a place. God gives man a name, a place, purpose and provision. It is what God does. But because of sin and iniquity things may change. The person who gave you the house has the power to reverse that whole thing; they can lock a person out. If you were not serving God when you got the house but now you serve God, Hallelujah, but the one who got you, gave you, or helped you get that house may be miffed and now may be coming for you. If you were serving God until you got that house, husband, or whatever you got from God and now you no longer serve God, you may be put out of that house just as Adam and Eve were put out of the Garden of Eden. The lock? A flaming sword that turned every which way.

Oh--, fire. Again. Fire.

was the power and authority of God... pretty much get out. The angel with the fire swords was the enforcement; those are the locks.

So, whoever got you or gave you the house, that's who holds the "mortgage." Have you paid them, spiritually speaking? Whoever gave you that house, have you paid them? Whoever you got the house (gift) from. You pay them with obedience and worship.

Did you dedicate it to God? Have you dedicated yourself to God? Gifts of God are given by God and given without repentance. A gift is given by Grace by His Mercy. Gifts of God are to be respected and treated a certain way. Additionally, you need to behave yourself a certain way. Somethings have conditions. Obedience to God and worship we remain in Christ.

The gifts of God are without repentance. Spiritual gifts are divine things. These are very high gifts. As well natural and physical gifts from God are also valuable gifts. This is why it could take so long for a person to get something, because when God gives, He gives. In the waiting period God is vetting, purging, God is changing, God is waiting for us to change, grow, develop, He may be waiting for us to *become*.

In some cases, God may be waiting for us to ask. Not just ask for a house, if that is what we want from Him, but to ask the

right question of God. He may be waiting for us to ask for the right thing, the right way.

I asked the Lord, "What must be ask for, if we are not asking for a house, when in the natural, we believe that is the thing we need--, a house?"

He said, "**Ask for the highest thing.**" Ask for the highest thing, not the highest priced thing, but the highest thing, and the lower stuff is already attached to that high thing. It is like wet comes with water. White comes with rice (well, white rice). Warmth comes with sunshine. Ask for the highest thing. Ask for the spiritual thing and the natural stuff comes with it or the natural stuff finds that spiritual thing.

The natural things will find the spiritual thing.

But if a man doesn't know who he is and his relationship with God he will not ask for the good and perfect and precious things, if he doesn't know he can have it. Or maybe he doesn't know that he can have it or doesn't believe he's good enough to get it or that he should receive it. Perhaps he doesn't believe he is good enough to God. Our Father created us in His own image and likeness and nothing can separate us from the His Love. If we ever had an Earthly model of that we could understand far better than if we never had an Earthly father who loved us unconditionally.

But to God the fact that you are asking for spiritual things indicates relationship and sonship. It means you want to be like Christ--, more like the Father and are not just trying to make a transaction to get things and stuff. Asking for Godly spiritual things is an indication of your awareness that you are a spirit, and you are spiritual, and that you are eternal. Transactional things are for today and for temporal purposes.

So, we may ask for the wrong thing the wrong way and maybe we get nothing.

Ye have not because ye ask not, or ye ask amiss. (James 4:3)

Because that may not be the way you ask for this thing that you want, that you know you need, that you believe you want. Maybe you are asking too simply.

In school, we learned about the lowest common denominator. That is useful information in the natural, but in the spirit, God is saying to ask for the highest thing. With God, ask for the highest from the Most High God, the highest, from the Lord of lords, the King of kings. Yes, God sits high and looks low, but God is spirit, so we must ask God for <u>spiritual</u> things and the natural things come with it--, you know those Blessings that come up and overtake you. When you receive the highest things, the lower things come right along with it.

Revelatory-- that the lack of something spiritual, some spiritual attribute could be the reason why we lack something in the natural. Selah--, think on that; meditate on that.

Now, we must know what natural things come with spiritual things, so we will know what spiritual things to ask for. It is not always as simple as a formula that works the same for everyone. It depends on your faith, who you are, your foundation, and your assigned destiny.

You may ask for a car. You don't ask for the car as individual parts, the carburetor, the tires, the doors, the steering wheel... but they all come with the car. By human nature, we consolidate that *ask* and take it up to the highest level of your understanding and ask for a car. But the Holy Spirit is the Spirit of Understanding so we must get help from the Holy Spirit to know what to ask for.

So, you may be asking for a car, but what if God is waiting for you to ask for an airplane or a jet? Then the highest level may be to ask for transportation. (God knows where you have to go.) He knows what type of vehicle should be supplied to you if you are asking for transportation.

Taking it into the spiritual, if you take it higher: ask God for Salvation, if you have not yet. You ask God for salvation which gets you in the right alignment with God. When you are in a son to loving Father, then you can ask Him anything. Ask God to fill you with the Holy Spirit because we will need

His assistance in knowing how to pray and what to ask for. Ask God for the Gifts of the Spirit that are appointed to you. Ask God to activate your gifts. Ask God to give you your Kingdom purpose and vision for it, in the Name of Jesus.

Then ask God for all the spiritual things required to do your spiritual assignment on Earth--, all things needed for life and godliness. if God allows, switch that to Godliness and life--, seek the Kingdom first. and mean it –.

After that, whatever else you ask for, such as a vehicle, will show up. Because you asked God for all the spiritual things. Your vehicle is the natural appendage, the natural thing attached to all those spiritual things that you have asked God for because you are spirit, God is Spirit and you are asking Him for spiritual things, which are eternal things, which are true riches.

Durable riches are in the hands of Wisdom.

> Riches and honour *are* with me; *yea,* durable riches and righteousness. (Proverbs 8:18)

Perhaps you don't even ask for the car, or a house. You ask for the spiritual things because blessings should be coming up to overtake you. Blessings that overtake? Yeah, it's the stuff you didn't ask for and weren't even expecting, but you get anyway.

> And all these blessings shall come on thee, and overtake thee, if thou shalt hearken unto the voice of the LORD thy God. (Deuteronomy 28:2)

> Long life is in her right hand; in her left hand are riches and honor. (Proverbs 3:16)

We don't ask God for riches or honor, we ask Him for Wisdom because Wisdom is the higher thing, spiritually. You want to live a long time? Ask God for Godly Wisdom. Ask for the spiritual thing. Ask for the Godly things.

Isaiah 11:2 describes the Spirit of the Lord that rests upon the Messiah, detailing seven attributes: Wisdom, Understanding, Counsel, Might, Knowledge, Fear of the Lord, and Delight in the Fear of the Lord. By the Holy Spirit we have access to these Spirits.

David asked the Lord not to take His Spirit away from him. (Psalm 51)

The Spirit of Counsel – no wise person in the Bible went to war or did anything of significance without Wise Counsel.

The Spirit of Might -many men of valor needed courage and might to enter into battle. They didn't just ask for it and pray for it, they sacrificed for it before going into battle. They built altars and sacrificed for what they wanted from the Lord. They asked for spiritual things.

The Spirit of Knowledge and Understanding - Daniel prayed for that along with Mercy. We should have the Fear of the Lord. We should pray for and expect that Goodness & Mercy will be following us all the days of our lives… (Psalm 23). In house ownership, Goodness and Mercy could play out as safety, as appliances lasting, or as storms not hitting your property. So, as God is watching the house, spiritual things that affect your property impact you favorably. Of course, you know the converse would be a result from the dark side.

These are spiritual things that we are asking for. With God, the natural things follow after because we are seeking first the Kingdom. Seeking God first. Has a blessing ever come up and overtaken you? This is being rich toward God.

With all your getting, get Understanding Proverbs 4:7. Yes, pray for understanding.

Wisdom is the principal thing; therefore get wisdom: and with all thy getting get understanding. (Proverbs 4:7)

Ask For Wholeness

When Jesus saw him lie, and knew that he had been now a long time in that case, he saith unto him, Wilt thou be made whole? (John 5:6)

Looking at this verse regarding this invalid man, Jesus asked him if he would like to be made whole. To me that means he could ask to be healed or ask to be made whole. Whole includes healing, but healing doesn't include wholeness. Healing comes with wholeness. Healing **finds** wholeness because the creation must obey the Word of God. When a man is made whole he is restored to God's original intent and design. Therefore, he must also be healed.

Being made whole is the highest thing. So, I asked the LORD what we should be asking for:

By the Holy Spirit I heard, **Ask for wholeness.**

- Ask for all that you've lost.
- All that has been stolen.
- All that you've been tricked out of.
- All that you bartered away (traded away).
- All that you have given away.
- All things that pertain to your wholeness.
- All that you never pursued to recover.
- Then ask for all that your ancestors lost, had stolen, tricked out of, bartered away, gave away, never pursued to recover.
- Then take a minute because that is a lot of stuff.

Then the Holy Spirit said, **"Go back to the Garden and to the beginning because you were created perfect."** You were created **perfect--**, that certainly echoed in my head. Man was created whole. By whole that means as a human you have everything you need to conduct your life successfully, even abundantly and amazingly. Knowing God, wouldn't that be how He would structure things and set a man up? To be blessed, victorious, successful. Surely God would not set His creation up to lose or be losers.

Nope, that would be devil-work.

Lucifer was not the only one created perfect as we would read in Ezekiel 28:12.

Man was created perfect. We need to look at the creation of man to even know what we should have and what could be missing and what we should be endeavoring to get back. *Beauty? Health? Comfort? Affluence? Abundance? A good reputation?* The Holy Spirit told me that is too low. That's what the Lord is telling me today: that is too low. Because we should be asking for <u>spiritual</u> things.

Man was formed: made in the image and likeness of God: What is that but perfection?

Life breathed into him and he became a living soul – not a fake soul, but a living soul and that is a soul plus a spirit.

Man was crowned and that means he is royalty. He has at least a princedom if not kingship because he was crowned. Even when a baby is being born the OB will see the baby's head and say, he is *crowning;* the top of the head is called the crown probably because that's how God made us and there is where a crown should sit. Just by being born in the Earth there are certain gifts, blessings, abilities and positions that re afforded and awarded to man.

- Man was crowned with glory. Amen.
- Man is crowned with honor. Amen.
- Man was given authority over the works all the works of God's hands.
- Man was set in dominion.
- Man was created a little lower than the Elohim--, a little lower than the angels, it says in some translations.

So, we were created perfect and **whole** <u>before the sin</u>, before the fall. When we sin, we fall, we lose parts of ourselves. We lose parts of our soul. And that is the purpose of sin it is to strip man of vital things that the devil wasn't to steal, or strip man of parts that the man needs to do his purpose and reach destiny. It is to strip man of his wholeness, so he is unsuccessful in life and purpose. That is always the purpose of sin— it is not so you can have fun or live dangerously, although fun might be the original perception. Sin can be fun, for a season. But the purpose of sin is to dismantle that man, his life, his glory, his wealth, his destiny. By so doing the devil desires to dismantle the plans of God for that man, for his family, his bloodline--, even for a nation, or the whole Earth, depending on that man's destined reach and Earthly assignment.

Our soul and the state and condition of it determine what kind of shape or condition the rest of us is in.

Really?

Yup, really.

Beloved I pray above all things that thou wouldest prosper and be in health even as your soul prospers. (1 John 2)

Your soul is a power pack. As soon as you sin, according to Apostle James Kawalya, the soul is fragmented into seven parts and each part is put in a different prison. Now, you are limping spiritually speaking because your soul, your life's power pack is diminished, lost, fragmented…or entirely gone.

We have been redeemed from the Curse of the Law, so everything we lost in the fall, we should be asking for those things back instead of continuing to fall and fall all over again. Every attribute and virtue, skill, ability, and endowment from God should be restored to us, unless we are already sin free and whole. Since redemption, if we have not collected our virtues and attributes back, we should be asking for those. After salvation, we should not be satisfied that we have a steering wheel, when we should have the whole car. With the steering wheel we think we are controlling where we are going. Are we? Where are the other parts of the vehicle?

With wholeness comes everything that pertains to our peace and everything we need for life and for Godliness. We were created perfect because God who is perfect made us.

Saints of God, you know the new baby smell – that's because that baby is formed perfectly and hasn't sinned yet. When man sins, things **die**. Cells die. Dying things smell different than living things. Even if by degrees.

When a flame has lost its spark, the flame dies down, it is not as bright as it was when it was fully aglow or fully ablaze. Flames die down.

Walking after the spirit you will not fulfill the lusts of the flesh. So, we don't sin, we don't die, we don't have cells that die or corrupt, or change. So, we will keep glowing and being bright—the candle of the Lord.

So, I challenge you, don't ask for anything after the flesh. Even though you hear preachers say, *Don't come to church unless you have a request of God.* I add, based on what the Holy Spirit told me, make sure that request is a spiritual request for a spiritual thing. If you ask for a natural or physical thing with no spiritual foundation or the wrong spiritual foundation backing for it, you either will not get it, will get a fake or imitation of it as the devil may step in to fulfill your order.

If you do happen to get what you want from God, without the proper spiritual backing, you may not be able to maintain or keep it. Most of us humans will think that just because we got what we wanted that it came from God.

Really? Discernment is critical to have. Ladies you get a husband and he turns out to be the worst thing that ever happened to you --, he wasn't from God, now was he?

In many ways this can be the Mercy of God. Have you ever noticed how people who hold onto things that cause them harm end up being lost or destroyed themselves? But if they let go of the accursed thing, they can be saved while the accursed thing is lost or removed. Bless your house and all that is in it, as well as the land it sits on, thereby destroying all evil covenants and reversing all curses involving your home and those who live in it.

Whle we are on the subject of spouses, bless your spouse. If they are from God the marriage and everyone in it will prosper. If he is not from God, you will know it sooner than later, but at least you did not curse your spouse.

Do not make a request of God if you are not fulfilling covenant because in that condition, you are out of authority. Being in covenant includes bringing a sacrifice for the altar. God hears by altars, He works by altars, and He answers by altars. Altars have bright flames, and they burn. What's at an altar? FIRE. God answers by Fire. God answers altars and He answers by altars--, by Fire.

No?

Yes.

God had Abraham to bring a sacrifice and prepare an altar. Sacrifices are burning 24/7 by the priests in the Old Testament. Double on Sabbaths and feast days. God had Jacob to build an altar – an altar is for the purpose of sacrifice. It is not just a monument, a sculpture or a piece of art.

> And Solomon offered a sacrifice of peace offerings, which he offered unto the Lord, two and twenty thousand oxen, and an hundred and twenty thousand sheep. (1 Kings 8:63)

Solomon offered a sacrifice of fellowship offerings to the Lord. He offered bullocks on the altar, twenty-two thousand cattle and a hundred and twenty thousand sheep and goats. So, the king and all the Israelites dedicated the temple of the Lord by sacrifice.

Did you dedicate your house to the Lord? What did you sacrifice? What did you give? Did you sacrifice prophetically, at the asking phase? Or, did you sacrifice to thank God and to dedicate the house or spouse or whatever you were asking God for?

God put Jesus on that Cross – that was an altar, and Jesus was the sacrifice in place of you and me. Jesus died so we could live. Only Jesus was pure enough to be a sacrifice.

So now we come to God, and we ask Him for things – spiritual things-- the things of real value. Eternal things. Spiritual things. True riches.

Temporal Things

In Jesus' temptation in the Wilderness, Jesus was offered earthly and temporal things. After all, what else did the devil have to offer Jesus that Jesus wouldn't see through? Man, regular man, on the other hand may not see through certain offerings if his discernment is not sharp and in use. For example, psychic knowledge which man seems to flock to like flies to honey is offered by the devil everyday and too many take the devil up on it because it is inherent in man to either want to or need to know things, such as the future. Any information coming from the devil is not to be relied on and should not be accepted. Yes, it is probably full of lies or may be partially true, but the spouting off or spewing out of those lies is also another deceptive trap—it is initiation because the devil you just got the information from you now owe them, and you have been initiated into the dark kingdom. If you never figure that out and never renounce the sin, then you're just in there. Now that you're in, your children are, and their children also are just in it. The devil's hold and escalation against your bloodline will simply increase over the generations if no one repents, renounces and asks God to get them out of the hell they got themselves into.

The devil could not offer Jesus such a thing, but mortal man---. Now you know.

The first temptation offering was food. But you have to make it yourself. Here is a food kit. Stone – turn it to bread yourself. Did Jesus need the devil to suggest a recipe for Him? Of course not.

If I were hungry I wouldn't tell you, I'd tell my Father who owns everything. If I were hungry, I would not tell thee: for the world is mine, and the fulness thereof. (Psalm 50:12)

He offered Jesus a thrill and power: Jump from the temple and the angels will save you. Satan doesn't even say I'll save you – he is just making work for God and God's angels. (Crazy)

The third temptation was for Fame, power, glory, money, the kingdoms of this world. Those things are temporal.

Temporal things are not high or highly spiritual things. And of course, they are not eternal.

> If therefore ye have not been faithful in the unrighteous mammon, who will commit to your trust the true *riches*? (Luke 16:11)

Money is not a destination; it is not a conclusion or a goal. You can look at it as an overtaking blessing, an *appendage* to Wisdom. Or, you can look at it as a test. It is not a conclusion or the end game; it is a test. On the one hand we don't want to be tested. I had a pastor who said he prayed every morning that the Lord not test him today. But we ask for money – and money is a test. Well, we are supposed to have it, but it is to show ourselves faithful so we can then be entrusted with **True Riches**.

And we are to be rich toward God. What are the true riches? The things that are about God, things that interest God, things that are important to God. Anything that is due unto God or resembles God in any way that is what it means to be like God. When we become more like Him, more conformed to the image in which we were created, when we were created PERFECT. Perfect and whole.

And he said unto them, Take heed, and beware of covetousness: for a man's life consisteth not in the abundance of the things which he possesseth.

And he spake a parable unto them, saying, The ground of a certain rich man brought forth plentifully:

And he thought within himself, saying, What shall I do, because I have no room where to bestow my fruits?

And he said, This will I do: I will pull down my barns, and build greater; and there will I bestow all my fruits and my goods.

And I will say to my soul, Soul, thou hast much goods laid up for many years; take thine ease, eat, drink, and be merry.

But God said unto him, Thou fool, this night thy **soul** shall be required of thee: then whose shall those things be, which thou hast provided?

So is he that layeth up treasure for himself, and is not rich toward God. (Luke 12:15-21)

Rich towards God means full of His counsels, interests, things due to him whatever can in any respect be likened unto God, or resemble him in any way. When we are conforming and transforming more and more like Him, like the Perfect Man. That is being rich toward God.

By Wisdom and discernment, a man must know whether to ask for things for now, in the temporal, or to ask for things for eternity. Because of our dual nature, spirit inhabiting a body... Spiritual things first: Seek **first** the Kingdom and all these things will be added.

> But seek ye first the kingdom of God, and his righteousness; and all these things shall be added unto you. (Matthew 6:33)

If we want the things before the Kingdom or the things instead of the Kingdom, that is when we open up wrong doors or wrong pathways and we create problems for ourselves or even others. So, if we keep asking for things, that is when the devil can sneak in and try to provide you with things. If you haven't sought the Kingdom first, as your foundation, those things could be gotten by you, and they could be attached to the devil, so now you are attached to the devil.

All the silver and the gold and the cattle on a thousand hills belongs to God. Have you noticed those things that belong to God, according to the Psalmist are all things that we use for sacrifice? That is true currency. But when we take currency and run off with it instead of using it as currency that is when mankind messes up. Royally. It's like getting a bag of seeds, but instead of planting it and then harvesting and getting more seed for next year, and for generations, you eat the seed.

Money is seed. Silver and gold represent money; they are seeds. Cattle on a thousand hills --- in the Old Testament, cattle were a lot of things, but it was seed. So, we should ask God for the means, the wherewithal, the thing that will cause us to get results, to create fruit and fruit that remains, not the seed that will create the fruit and then eat the fruit, instead of submitting it to the Godly process. When man only wants the pleasure without the process – that's what got Onan killed.

Jesus, in the Wilderness had just gotten baptized by John the Baptist in the Jordan River. The Spirit of God had just descended on Him, like a dove. And a voice from Heaven had just said, "This is My Son, in whom I Am well pleased."

Saints of God, Jesus received the Kingdom of Heaven. **first**, before the temptation. Seeking things *before* the Kingdom is when the when the purveyor of **things--**, the devil steps in to provide and tempt you. Usually, the person who keeps asking for things, hasn't sought the Kingdom of God, first; they are steeped in their flesh life. That person is more temptable, more lustful, spiritually weaker. In that condition, *things* are the temptation. If you receive from the devil or any of his agents and you don't have the Kingdom either shoring you up because you went through the process or backing you up because the Kingdom has your back, you will be in a world of trouble.

Bypass the Devil

If we ask for the right stuff, we bypass the devil completely because he doesn't have the spiritual things that we are asking **God** for.

He's got copies or if you are about to get something from God, the devil may put up a roadblock, but the devil for instance has no Mercy, he has no Fruit of the Spirit. Ask for spiritual things, ask for loftier things, ask for high things. The devil has pre-processed stuff, pre-packaged stuff. It is the spiritually or otherwise lazy man who doesn't want to submit to the *process* of a thing to get the correct results. He just wants the results, only. The man who plants the seed, goes through the seasons and then harvests is following the *process* of a thing. Yes, he may take his harvest to market and now he has money.

The lazy, instant man cares nothing of the process and he just wants the money. Enter the devil. Even though the devil will try to get into and interrupt the process, he ultimately wants to offer shortcuts, the way to bypass the process.

Daniel asked God for Wisdom, Knowledge, Understanding & Mercy. In Daniel 2:17-18, Daniel seeks Mercy from God to reveal the interpretation of King Nebuchadnezzar's dream. And Daniel is asking for Understanding of Visions: In Daniel 9:20-23, Daniel prays for insight regarding the future of his people and Jerusalem. So, ask for high things, and for things that are for more than just for yourself. Selfish things are not high things.

> Ye ask, and receive not, because ye ask amiss, that ye may consume *it* upon your lusts.(James 4:3)

Nowhere in the Bible did God send a man to Earth to be exalted and to live his best life, just for himself. Jesus didn't even come to make a name for Himself. So, if your prayers, purpose, and goals do not include others, then who sent you? Did you send yourself? Or is the devil somehow involved in your goals?

If your vision for your life is limited to what you see in the mirror and that alone, you are out of order. Your spiritual vision determines what you ask for.

If you have no spiritual vision, then you will ever be asking for natural things. Selfish things. Temporal things. Near-sighted things because you can't see far down the road.

That's the realm of the devil--, that **near realm.** Especially that selfish realm. You hungry? Here's a stone, and a food kit: **Hello Flesh.** Go ahead, turn that stone into bread. *Me, me, me.* The devil is prince this world, and he can interfere with or intercept flesh prayers and prayers for only natural and soulish things. Soulish prayers. That near now, immediate and desperate realm. Without faith it is impossible to please God. Faith is the substance of things hoped for, and the evidence of things not seen. One evidence is believing that God is and that is a rewarder of those that diligently seek Him. Another evidence is your behavior while you wait on God. Patience and every other Fruit of the Spirit is evidence of faith. So, time is involved and how you behave yourself in that time, in that meanwhile is evidence of your faith.

Vision: Wilderness. God is giving Israelites manna in the morning (Exodus 16). Enough for today only. (double on the Sabbath) Well, of course He wasn't too happy with them at that point. He was rationing their provision. If God is rationing your provision, then you need to be praying real hard right now. Repenting.

In the and they were behaving very poorly in their circumstances. They were walking, and 11-day trip, making it last 40 years – they were behaving very poorly. God already knew they were not going to get into the Promised Land. And then, rationed provisions? Very scary. It's like death row. God gave them plenty of chances, but it was like a multitude of people in a perp walk headed to Death Row.

Repent! With fasting and praying.

Ever notice you get more flies with honey than with vinegar? Ever notice that even your own parents will give you more and sooner if you have a good attitude and a good behavior than not. Because of their behavior, or lack of it, their lack of evident faith, God was repenting saving them anyway. But if God is rationing your provision, then you need to be praying – repenting real hard right now.

The devil can't get in unless there is an open door, find out where it is and close it. If the devil is interfering in what God is giving you, then you need to be fasting and praying now to God, starting with repentance. The devil can't get in unless there is a door open.

Increase in Spiritual Vision

Your prayer is that God will increase your spiritual vision. When you can see into the spirit, more into the spirit, deeper into the spirit, further into the spirit you will know what to pray for and not just for today.

Of course, *give us this day, our daily bread* is how Jesus taught the disciples to pray. But He was just teaching them to pray, meaning they didn't know how to pray, hadn't prayed at all yet, or weren't sure they were praying right at all. So they were just praying for today rather beginner-*ish*. But that doesn't mean that is we've been in Christ for a while, a seasoned Christian that we just pray for today.

Who Got You That House?

Now. I'm saying all this because you or your ancestors – whoever got that house that you live in may have asked God for a house. Whoever got you that house that you might be living in, we must look at their spiritual condition soberly. That's well and good as long as they first sought the Kingdom of Heaven

Not accusing anyone of anything. I'm looking at myself too, right now. Thank You, Holy Spirit. What is the history of house-getting in your family or bloodline? Did your dad get the family a house and keep it nice and mow the lawn every week? I'd say that man is doing a lot more than what you see in the natural. In the spirit that man is establishing a spiritual standard for that bloodline. Actually, he may not be just establishing it, he may be following through from his father's standard and his *father's* father's standard.

First houses. Do nothing. Don't know what to do. Don't have the means to do. Barely making it or maintaining. This goes back to vision. When the man with the good history of house-getting, house-living, house-maintaining, and eventually house-selling, or house-transference, either by selling or leaving to his generations thinks of buying a house he envisions all that.

When the desperate man thinks of a house, his vision is more limited. He needs shelter and he needs it today. How much for a house? The man with vision, how much for a house and perhaps by experience, knowledge, understanding, and vision he may also ask, how much to maintain it? How much to keep it? How much to keep it nice so when I sell it, there is a profit.

Vision.

Walk or ride around your own neighborhood, you will see the difference just in the appearance of the yard or the paint or lack of paint on the shutters.

Who, and in what circumstances did that person acquire that house?

You've asked God for a house that is well and good if the Kingdom was already sought first and you asked God for anything – Jesus said Ask the Father, anything in My Name, then God gave you that thing, that house. As long as you opened the door and let Jesus in, then He dwells there and nobody and nothing can displace you from the house that God gave you. I am saying that because we are Christians.

Unfortunately, on the dark side those who get things from the dark side if they keep serving their idol *gods* they may maintain their lifestyle, unless and until God passes judgment on it. God will not always wink at the evil that men do.

What's In the Kingdom?

The Kingdom of Heaven provides, Wisdom, Knowledge, Understanding, Counsel, Might, Fear of the Lord, Vision, Mercy, Grace, Truth, many virtues of God. The true riches.

Seek first the kingdom and all these other things will be added to you. (Matthew 11:12)

With spiritual vision, you pray differently. You prepare differently.

This book is about being locked out – and I am going by the leading of the Holy Spirit. It's about having a home, buying a home, keeping a home, living in a home, staying in a home--, ultimately, it is about having home-security and passing that security into your bloodline.

It's about not being locked out.

In the Parable of the Ten Virgins (Matthew 25:1–13), ten virgins are waiting for the bridegroom so they can join the wedding feast. Five are wise and bring extra oil for their lamps; five are foolish and do not. When the bridegroom finally arrives-- at night, the foolish virgins' lamps have gone out, so they leave to buy more oil. Of course it's night because if the Kingdom is not there, there is no Light. (The foolish virgins didn't have the Kingdom because foolishness is counter to Kingdom – *ness*.)

While they are gone, the bridegroom arrives, the wise virgins enter the feast and the door is shut. They can't get back in.

This is about anointing, prayer, light is trimmed, and your light is aglow, it is ablaze. So, you don't have to leave off what you are doing. You are prepared; you have prepared.

The foolish virgins return and plead, "Lord, Lord, open the door for us!"

He replies, "Truly I tell you, I don't know you."

If you'd been up to the Throne of God for worship, and in prayer then He'd know you. He won't have to say, "I don't know you." If you had been in prayer that is where anointing is gained. The oil is the anointing. So you will have enough oil to trim your lamp and be aglow. They went through the trouble of being virgins, they weren't even sexually immoral but still got locked out. Be prepared and observe the disciplines of faith.

In our Christian walk we have be both prepared and also observe the disciplines of the faith.

Had they known, had the known when (no man knows the day or the hour) so had they by faith believed that the Lord would return, that is spiritual vision and by faith, they would have prepared. Well, half of them did.

God told Noah that He was sending a flood (Genesis 7:16). Spiritual vision sometimes means also having spiritual **ears**, for we don't walk by sight but by faith and faith comes by hearing. Noah prepared differently than all the other people… who didn't prepare at all.

God shut the door of the ark after Noah, his family, and the animals entered. The others couldn't get into that house of safety. Everyone outside was permanently shut out from safety once the floodwaters surged.

Being locked out of something you thought you had access to, or something that you thought you owned, or locked out and not being able to get something that you would like to own – that's being locked out as well. Seek first the Kingdom, and all of its Righteousness. You've done that, *right*?

Jesus told the woman at the well – if you knew what kind of water I have...

The point is and the subject is being locked out of something that you thought you owned, or locked out of, or not able to get something that you'd like to own.

It could be that some wayward ancestor is the cause of the lock out. Why do people in your family not have houses? Why do they not have certain *kinds* of houses, such as nice houses? Why are houses gotten but then lost in a family or bloodline? Why is there house insecurity in your family, or bloodline? This speaks of any type of house, apartment, condo, townhouse, single family home. Is there a familial pattern to the housing problem you may be having? Is there housing insecurity in your family? Are some or all of you stressed out about rent and mortgage payments all the time?

If everyone else is okay and it is only you and everyone else legitimately has a house, then it it's you. REPENT.

More Money

The most obvious and near-sighted answer to anything is money. If there was more money. Money answers a lot of things, but remember, money is an end product, but not the final goal. Money is often a test. Do you recognize money as seed, or as a *god*? Money is a little g *god* – Mammon, but it is not the highest. It is not the highest power, God is the highest power. Money is actually the lowest power on Earth. And we are supposed to be showing God our ability to have dominions and control over it and that it doesn't have control over us.

So why is there still housing insecurity? Some people have money, but they may still have housing insecurity, maybe their credit rating is jacked. Maybe they can't get into the house they want, or any house.

A person with a spiritual issue regarding houses could be given a house and they may still find a way to mess up things. They could misbehave and get kicked out. They could cheat on their spouse and one or both get kicked out. Any number of things, including the house getting torn down itself. I know a woman who had a very good dental practice, suddenly, she didn't have a place to practice because the city condemned the building where her long-time practice was located. She had just lost her primary living abode due to a divorce. See, that's a spiritual problem either of hers, or maybe someone else in that complex, and she was collateral damage. Or maybe in that city. Perhaps the city was decaying—there could have been spiritual territorial issues or a judgement was called on that area because of rampant sin. These are all things to commit to prayer. For best results, stay prayed up.

Why are their housing difficulties in a family or in a bloodline? Could be the foundation. Could be the ancestors let in certain spiritual locksmith that locked out future generations. That could be what is inhibiting your generations or multiple generations of your bloodline from being able to have a home.

They could have sinned. Didn't repent. Passed iniquity into the bloodline into the foundation. Allowed doors to be opened. Made devil deals and once such evil deal could have had a tiny line item in the evil covenant that the family doesn't get to own land, property, or houses.

And you're born an innocent, cute little baby, smelling good, and you have no idea that is what will be looking for you when you look for a place to live or a house to buy or just to live in 20 years from now. How have your ancestors handled houses and living situations? Whatever your ancestors have *allowed* has been released into your foundation and your bloodline.

When you hear a person say I'm the first person in my family to have a house, that is a huge statement. Yes we can celebrate – that is if that man sought first the Kingdom and that's how he got his home. And that man endeavored to stay in the Kingdom. If he did not, then there will be struggle after struggle, like a cursed life regarding the house and all things related to it.

It could be in that covenant that this group gets houses, but someone takes them, tears them up, steals them, burns them down or floods sweep them away. Except the Lord watch that house, those who watch --, watch in vain.

> Unless the LORD builds the house, those who build it labor in vain. Unless the LORD watches over the city, the watchman stays awake in vain. (Psalm 127:1 ESV)

You may have lots of spiritual work to do. Because mostly you don't know, most of us probably don't know what the folks who came before us did and what mess they left us to sort out or suffer through. Maybe they didn't give a thought at all, just selfish, thinking of themselves and what they wanted. Their vision may have been desperation, which is not vision, but simple declared, *"I need a house. I need a place for my family."*

Maybe your ancestors weren't spiritual. Maybe they were spiritual to the dark side...and made devil deals. Getting what they wanted for right then, not caring about future generations.

Start with repentance. First for yourself and then go all the way down your bloodline. I'd go back to Adam and Eve for best results.

You don't want to be just standing outside, or standing at a gate looking at a house that you can't have. Don't let the door close on you. If you find the doors closed and you know you should have a house, deserve a house, or that God has promised you a house and you know your right relationship with God, then don't let that door or any doors stay closed on you. If not for you, do the warfare for the sake of your children and your generations.

In our temporal, finite, human minds we may always think if we have more money we can have this that or the other. It may not be true; everything is not for sale. Naboth didn't sell his vineyard to Ahab, now, did he?

Even if you have the money, where you got the money? Being money doesn't make it consecrated, until you consecrate all our gain to the Lord God.

This is the house that Jack built—nursery rhyme Jack built a house then this happened and then the next thing--, the cat and the dog. All kinds of things can happen when God is not in a thing. So you've got money? Okay--, but it depends on where and how you go the money. What *god* were you serving when you got that house? What *god* were you serving when you got that money? What *god* were you serving when you got that job that got you that money that got you the house? It depends a lot on all of that, *Jack*.

If you had more money, **and** that money came from God **and** is consecrated to God. That determines what you get, when you get it how you get it, if you get to enjoy it, how long you get to keep it. Where's the enjoyment of living in a beautiful home but you are stressing every night about mortgage, maintenance and payments instead of enjoying it?

If whatever you get, you don't get from God, it is only temporary. You may enjoy it in your generation, but what about your kids? If you got it in the wrong way there could be a curse waiting to blindside your kids if you got it selfishly.

    A man went to sleep one night. In the dream the Lord told him (I think he said angel) told him who to go see and how much money to take that man to get a certain plot of land. The man did what he was instructed in the dream. The man bought the land, built a house for his family and they lived there for many years, and he has descendants who still live there. The house stood for nearly 100 years until one of the grandchildren decided it wasn't a good house anymore and lit a match to it and burned it down.

    Was there a 100-year covenant in some fine print with this man? We don't know, but we do know that his older children and their children prospered house-wise, but one son didn't and neither did that one son's children prosper regarding houses and house-security.

    That man got a house after his wife nagged and forced him to. That man did no upkeep on the house that he got. The wife constantly said that when she was dead and gone that the house would fall down. Years after that wife passed, that house burned down, by suspicious means and later it was bulldozed – that house fell down. Well, it was knocked down. After that for no particular reason the house was buried, purposely by that bulldozer operator at the request of an in-law who hired the dozer.

42. Lord, anything of mine that has been buried, anything that relates to me, my future, my prosperity, my children, their children, my generation and bloodline that has been buried, send mighty angels of God to unearth it today, in the Name of Jesus.

43. Earth O Earth always bear favorable witness of me and my family, in the Name of Jesus.

44. Lord, do not let that burial be prophetic or symbolic as it pertains to the housing situation of my bloodline, in the Name of Jesus.

Gifts of God Are Without Repentance

If you don't get what you want from God, then it is temporal. You may enjoy it in your generation but what about your kids? What about their kids? If whatever you get is not from God there is a hefty price to pay—either now or later or now and later.

> For the gifts and calling of God are without repentance. (Romans 11:29)

Job said the Lord giveth and the Lord taketh away (Job 1:21). God didn't say that; Job did. Job thought that all the devil was doing to him was God doing those things – Job was not right; Job was wrong. Job was not God. Job spoke as a finite mortal man, not as the eternal oracles of God.

When God gives you something He gives it to you. when He gifts your bloodline, He gifts it. It is there. When you by warfare or by Grace have something that was previously lost from your bloodline restored again--, you simply have it. It is yours to lose again or yours to keep. There are conditions in our Christian walk. We can do things to lose it, but God doesn't just decide I don't want them to have that anymore, I think I'll take it away. No, people fall under judgment, so there is a reason something may be taken away, but as long as you stay in the will of God, what He gives you, you can keep it, and God will even help you keep it.

The devil comes not but to steal, kill and destroy (John 10:10)

God may allow judgments if there is sin and iniquity. but He doesn't lie, His gifts are without repentance, and He doesn't steal.

So, what should we ask God for in order to be homeowners and landowners? What do we ask for to be people who enjoy homes and live in them and can pass them into their generations? **We should be asking for wholeness**. Ask Him for all that has been lost so you can again be restored to wholeness. Ask Him for all that has been stolen from you so you can be restored.

By virtue of who made us and how we are made, all those things are built in. They are automatic. God gives us a name, a place, provision automatically. We only lose them when we lose **spiritual things**. We lose the natural things that come with the spiritual things that we have lost. Those are the things that happen when the Earth brings thorns and thistles and hardship by the Curse of the Law. Which comes after sin, after getting kicked out of the house. What we may have gained or lost is reflective of the condition of our spirit man and our own souls.

Adam got kicked out of the house and men after him have suffered housing problems. So, when you pray, when you repent, go back all the way to Adam and Eve. What your father allowed, incurred, or released is still alive if you haven't done anything about it. If you still look like your father, then the same things will keep happening to you, no matter how much you don't want to be like him. It doesn't matter how much you want to break the mold and the curse, if you don't do the spiritual work, the curse won't just break. You have to break it. Put in the work.

Jesus asked: Will you be made whole? Reiterating, by the Holy Spirit I heard,

- Ask for wholeness.
- Ask for all that you've lost.
- All that has been stolen.
- All that you've been tricked out of.
- All that you bartered (traded away).
- All that you have given away.
- All things that pertain to your wholeness.
- All that you never pursued to recover.
- All that your ancestors lost, had stolen, tricked out of, bartered away, gave away, never pursued to recover.

Then take a minute because that is a lot of stuff. You may need to write this down – the Holy Spirit may download a lot of stuff to you.... write it down so it will help you pray. Don't let the door close on you. Don't let it stay closed.

So, when God opens a door for you to get a house, buy a house, have a house, live in a house, no man can close it, as long as you remain in God. Unless you are that man who does not continue to walk upright before the Lord.

When you begin to look like Jesus, like the Perfect Man (in Christ) then all the things that belong to the perfect man will obey and come to find that man. The blessings of the Lord maketh rich and he adds no sorrow. All these blessings will come up and overtake you.

Don't let the door close on you. God opens doors no man can close. So, stay in Christ. Continue the obedience, worship and follow the disciplines of the faith. Get a house, have a house, live in a house. Walk upright before the Lord.

Human Error

God gives gifts without repentance, but by human error, the enemy may have an open door to come to take what you have. By disaster, plague, famine, flood fire, the enemy may send something to take away what you have. But if God is watching the house, then you are not watching in vain.

God shuts doors in judgment if there is iniquity and sin without repentance. But God can open doors of blessings. And when He opens them, no man, no demon, no circumstance can close them. As long as you are in Christ and you have sought first the Kingdom of Heaven.

That means that if you got your house from God and you remain in good standing with the Lord, then you're fine. No worries. God can even give you a house you didn't build, it is part of those blessings that come up and overtake you. In Deuteronomy 6:10-

11 the Canaanites were displaced and the Israelites inherited houses.

If you didn't get your house from God, but by some other way, then you've got work to do. Afterward, make sure your house is dedicated to God. People lost houses in the Bible. Babylon conquered Israel and burned down their houses. Worse, they were taken captive into Babylon. (2 Kings 25, Jeremiah 6:12).

By Judgment of God, Job's kids lost their houses and their lives (Job 1:12). Their houses fell on them. Also, by the judgement of God, the houses of the wicked will be destroyed, (Proverbs 14:11, Zephaniah 1:13).

Enemies of God may come by battles and wars and **conquests** and take things that belong to others, such as houses. This is why you must continually pay attention to the things of God. Being rich toward God. Because when a person is not paying attention or has no spiritual vision is as good as blind or lost.

God may have shown you something spiritually important in a dream, but it was ignored. Not seeing the night vision **as** a vision and like Daniel praying for interpretation of the vision. Daniel prayed for 21 days for interpretation. If you pray for 5 minutes and don't get the interpretation, don't let it go.

By God's **Judgment** (taken by God's decree) because of sin, idolatry or some other work of the flesh a door of provision, prosperity, or blessing could be closed on you.

By evil human agents, or other entities, manipulation, mischief, demonics, witchcraft--, curses, evil doors may be opened, but only by giving permission by sinning. With sin and iniquity in you **without** repentance there is a way for the curse to alight.

There could be other ways to lose out, but if you seek God and the Kingdom, God will set you free. God can turn curses to blessings.

Debt in the natural starts out as spiritual debt—sin debt, iniquity. Look closely in your life, family or bloodline to see if there is sin debt hovering that is inviting and causing the hardship of debt in the natural realm. It could be something your family even still does that seems like nothing, but it may be sin. Unforgiveness? Jealousy? Covetousness are often the culprits. Deal accordingly.

Manipulation can be another. Why is anyone manipulating the life of another? Control, domination, intimidation – those are all witchcraft. Spiritual sabotage comes through temptation. Temptation leads to sin, even if by trickery. Bye-bye, house.

Pride and demonic stubbornness kept the nation of Egypt trapped in bondage. Pharaoh's hardened heart against Israel (Exodus 5–14). All those little g *gods* Pharoah and the Egyptians were worshipping – surely that territory was next to or impossible to get out of--, unless and until God brought them out. God set His people free. Amen.

Balaam's curse against Israel originally wouldn't land, (Numbers 22–24; 31:16; Revelation 2:14). Balaam couldn't curse Israel directly, so he counseled Balak to lure them into idolatry and immorality, which brought God's judgment and stalled their forward movement. (Witchcraft can't work unless there is a cause for the curse to alight – sin/iniquity) stay repentant before the Lord.

The purpose of sin is to curse a man.

Paul said he wanted to come to Thessalonica but he was hindered by Satan (1 Thessalonians 2:18) Paul wanted to visit the believers in Thessalonica, but said, "Satan hindered us." Sometimes you've got to do warfare, praying, fasting, set up an altar to overcome forces of darkness.

Unseen spiritual interference can close the doors of many kinds, as in territorial powers or principalities. So, like Daniel, fast pray, seek the Lord. greater door of influence. A great and effectual door --- sometimes strongmen must be defeated so you can get what God has for you.

Look carefully and prayerfully at what we are agreeing to or aligning ourselves with, so we don't lock ourselves out of houses and other blessings of the Lord. Demonic deception can work if there is lack of discernment or lack of seeking God.

Except for the Mercy of God, it has often worked. Israelites made a covenant with Gibeonites and then God couldn't help them. Making wrong alliances, joining up with the wrong crowd can affect your daily life and living and also your destiny.

We must be wise so that the enemy doesn't lock us out of house or houses. I say that because what if your business or career involved **owning several houses**? Or, what if your destiny involved you owning, moving to, or living in more than one house, if not simultaneously, perhaps sequentially? What if you are supposed to be ministering three cities over next, but you can't move from where you are because of an upside-down mortgage, or your credit has deteriorated for whatever reason, and you are stuck and can't move?

You do see how serious this is, right? Look very carefully and prayerfully regarding what you sign or agree to. Think **spiritually**, not just judging situations by what you see or hear.

The Kingdom of Heaven suffereth violence and the violent take it by force. (Matthew 11:12)

    Don't help the enemy lock you out of your own blessings including your house or houses. Sometimes the door closes because the enemy fights us. Sometimes it closes because we walk into a trap without asking God first. Either way, the lesson is clear: seek **<u>first</u>** the Kingdom.

Ask For the Highest Spiritual Thing

Ask for the highest thing, spiritually speaking. Ask for the highest spiritual thing because you are a highly created spiritual being – created a little lower than the Elohim (the angels some versions say). Pray before you act, discern before you agree, and trust God to open what no man can shut. Trust God to close what no man can open.

That's how you get your house, that's how you keep your house and everything else you get from God.

Some doors may slam in your face if the enemy is fighting you, but do the work. Battle, do the warfare; stand and stand therefore declaring to the enemy that he cannot take what God has promised you--, what God has given you. Amen.

doors may close because you walked into the wrong agreement, the wrong relationship, or the wrong opportunity without asking God first repent and get out of those wrong relationships because they put you in wrong timelines for your life. This may cause a person to miss the opportunities that God has for you. The chips may be stacked against you because of an evil or ignorant ancestor while you were born innocent and blameless. If you see this pattern in your family you've got a lot of work to do.

If Jesus is standing at the door of your house or the door of your heart and you have not given Him access or it's not His house because of how you got it, you have repentance to do and changes to make.

Whatever you get, get it from God or there is too much to pay, and the enemy cannot be trusted not to come and steal it or just take it away. Get everything from God and no other way, this way you don't owe any other entities, demons, devils or idol *gods*. Make sure God has given you that house and also that heart, that heart of flesh. So, if the door must shut, let it be against the enemy not against you.

If you are not saved; fix that.

Dedicate yourself, your life, and your house and home to the Lord today. Remember, God is not mocked, you can't trick Him into giving you what you want and then go back to your old, sinful lifestyle.

Ask God for spiritual things and the natural things will naturally seek you.

No longer will they build houses for others to inhabit, nor plant for others to eat. For as is the lifetime of a tree, so will be the days of My people, and My chosen ones will fully enjoy the work of their hands. (Isaiah 65:22)

God bless you.

I seal these words, these decrees and declarations across every timeline and dimension, every age and era past present and future and to infinity in the Name of Jesus. I seal them with the Blood of Jesus and the Holy Spirit of Promise.

Let every retaliation against this speaker, these words, the listeners and anyone who will pray these prayers at any time in the future backfire against the perpetrators without Mercy and to infinity, in the Name of Jesus. **Amen.**

Dear Reader

      Thank you for acquiring and reading this book. Thank you for supporting this ministry.

Keys to Your New House: And Everything Else, *(The)* is the companion book to Don't Tear Down Your Own House as it it rounds up the teachings on the house, the lock, and the keys.

Shalom,

Dr. Marlene Miles

Prayerbooks by this author

While most books by this author have prayer points either throughout the book or at the end, there are some books that are only prayers. You just open up the book and pray.

Prayers Against Barrenness: *For Success in Business and Life*

Fruit of the Womb: *Prayers Against Barrenness*

Beauty Curses, *Warfare Prayers Against*
https://a.co/d/5Xlc20M

Courts of Marriage: Prayers for Marriage in the Courts of Heaven *(prayerbook)*
https://a.co/d/cNAdgAq

Courtroom Warfare @ Midnight
(prayerbook) https://a.co/d/5fc7Qdp

Demonic Cobwebs *(prayerbook)*
https://a.co/d/fp9Oa2H

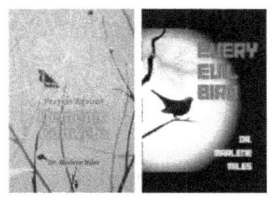

Every Evil Bird https://a.co/d/hF1kh1O

Gates of Thanksgiving

I AM NOT YOUR TARGET: *Warfare Against Haters & the Powers They Employ*

Spirits of Death, Hell & the Grave, Pass Over Me and My House

Throne of Grace: Courtroom Prayer

Warfare Prayer Against Poverty
https://a.co/d/bZ61lYu

Other books by this author

AK: The Adventures of the Agape Kid

Already Married in the Spirit: *Why You May Not Be Married in the Natural*

AMONG SOME THIEVES
https://a.co/d/dkYT4ZV

Ancestral Powers

Anti-Marriage, *The Spirit of*

Backstabbers https://a.co/d/gi8iBxf

Barrenness, *Prayers Against* https://a.co/d/feUltIs

Battlefield of Marriage, *The*

Beware of the Dog: Prayers Against Dogs in the Dream.

Bless Your Food: *Let the Dining Table be Undefiled*

Blindsided: *Has the Old Man Bewitched You?* https://a.co/d/5O2fLLR

Break Free from Collective Captivity

Broken Spirits & Dry Bones

By Means of a Whorish Father https://a.co/d/7UEB7te

Casting Down Imaginations

Churchzilla, The Wanna-Be, Supposed-to-be Bride of Christ

Demonic Cobwebs (prayerbook)

Demonic Time Bombs

Demons Hate Questions

Devil Loves Trauma, *The*

Devil Weapons: Unforgiveness, Bitterness,...

The Devourers: Thieves of Darkness 2

Do Not Swear by the Moon

Don't Refuse Me, Lord (4 book series) <u>https://a.co/d/idP34LG</u>

Dream Defilement

The Emptiers: *Thieves of Darkness, 1* <u>https://a.co/d/5I4n5mc</u>

Evil Touch

Failed Assignment

Fantasy Spirit Spouse <u>https://a.co/d/hW7oYbX</u>

FAT Demons (The): *Breaking Demonic Curses* <u>https://a.co/d/4kP8wV1</u>

The Fold (5-book series)
- The Fold (Book 1)
- Name Your Seed (Book 2)
- The Poor Attitudes of Money (3)
- Do Not Orphan Your Seed (4)
- For the Sake of the Gospel (5)

- My Sowing Journal

Gang Ups: Touch Not God's Anointed

Getting Rid of Evil Spiritual Food

https://a.co/d/i2L3WYQ

got HEALING? Verses for Life

got LOVE? Verses for Life

got HOPE? Verses for Life

got money? https://a.co/d/g2av41N

Here Come the Horns: *Skilled to Destroy*
https://a.co/d/cZiNnkP

Hidden Sins: Hidden Iniquity

https://a.co/d/4Mth0wa

How to Dental Assist

How to Dental Assist2: Be Productive, Not Wasteful

How to STOP Being a Blind Witch or Warlock

I AM NOT YOUR TARGET: *Warfare Against Haters and the Powers they Employ*

I Take It Back

Keepsakes or Mistakes:

Keys to Your New House: And Everything Else, *(The)*

Legacy

Let Me Have A Dollar's Worth
https://a.co/d/h8F8XgE

Level the Playing Field

Living for the NOW of God

Lose My Location
https://a.co/d/crD6mV9

Love Breaks Your Heart

Made Perfect In Love

Mammon https://a.co/d/29yhMG7

Man Safari, *The*

Marriage Ed. Rules of Engagement & Marriage

Made Perfect in Love

Money Hunters: Beware of Those

Money on the Altar https://a.co/d/4EqJ2Nr

Mulberry Tree, *The*
https://a.co/d/9nR9rRb

Motherboard (The) - *Soul Prosperity Series*

Name Your Seed

Occupy: *Until I Return*
https://a.co/d/bZ7ztUy

Plantation Souls

Players Gonna Play

Portals: Shut the Front Door: Prayers to Close Evil Portals.

Power Money: Nine Times the Tithe

https://a.co/d/gRt41gy

The Power to Get Wealth
https://a.co/d/e4ub4Ov

Powers Above

The Robe, Part 1, The Lessons of Joseph

The Robe, Part II, The Lessons of Joseph

Seasons of Grief

Seasons of Waiting

Seasons of War

Second Marriage, Third--, *Any Marriage*

https://a.co/d/6m6GN4N

Seducing Spirits: Idolatry & Whoredoms

https://a.co/d/4Jq4WEs

Shut the Front Door: *Prayers to Close Portals* https://a.co/d/cH4TWJj

Sift You Like Wheat

Six Men Short: What Has Happened to all the Men?

SLAVE

Soul Prosperity soul prosperity series 3

https://a.co/d/5p8YvCN

Souls Captivity soul prosperity series 2

The Spirit of Anti-Marriage

The Spirit of Poverty
https://a.co/d/abV2o2e

Spiritual Thieves https://a.co/d/eqPPz33

StarStruck- Triangular Power series.

SUNBLOCK- Triangular Power series.

The Swallowers: *Thieves of Darkness*, 3

Take It Back

This Is NOT That: How to Keep Demons from Coming at You

Time Is of the Essence

Too Many Wives: *Why You Have Lady Problems*

Tormenting Spirits
https://a.co/d/dAogEJf

Toxic Souls

Triangular Power *(series)*

- Powers Above
- SUNBLOCK
- Do Not Swear by the Moon
- STARSTRUCK

Unbreak My Heart: *Don't Let Me Die*

Uncontested Doom

Unguarded Hours, *The*

Unseen Life, *The* (forthcoming)

Upgrade: How to Get Out of Survival Mode

- Toxic Souls (Book 2 of series)
- Legacy (Book 3 of series)

The Wasters: *Thieves of Darkness,* Bk 2
https://a.co/d/bUvI9Jo

What Have You to Declare? What Do You Have With You from Where You've Been?

When I Was A Child, *I Prayed As a Child*

When the Devourer is Rebuked

https://a.co/d/1HVv8oq

The Wilderness Romance *(series)* This series is about conducting a Godly relationship and marriage with someone who is a Wilderness person. It is about how to recognize it and navigate through it. These books are about how not to get caught up in such.

- *The Social Wilderness*
- *The Sexual Wilderness*
- *The Spiritual Wilderness*

Other Series

The Fold (a series on Godly finances)
https://a.co/d/4hz3unj

Soul Prosperity Series https://a.co/d/bz2M42q

Spirit Spouse books

https://a.co/d/9VehDSo

https://a.co/d/97sKOwm

Battlefield of Marriage, The

https://a.co/d/eUDzizO

Players Gonna Play

https://a.co/d/2hzGw3N

Sent Spirit Spouse (can someone send you a spirit spouse? This book is not yet released.)

Matters of the Heart

Made Perfect in Love
https://a.co/d/7OMQW3O

Love Breaks Your Heart
https://a.co/d/4KvuQLZ

Unbreak My Heart
https://a.co/d/84ceZ6M

Broken Spirits & Dry Bones
https://a.co/d/e6iedNP

Thieves of Darkness series

The Emptiers https://a.co/d/heio0dO

The Wasters https://a.co/d/5TG1iNQ

The Swallowers https://a.co/d/1jWhM6G

The Devourers: Why We Can't Have Nice Things https://a.co/d/87Tejbf

Spiritual Thieves

Triangular Powers https://a.co/d/aUCjAWC

Upgrade (series) ***How to Get Out of Survival Mode*** https://a.co/d/aTERhX0

Links for You Tube Prayers:

Repentance https://www.youtube.com/watch?v=RogSEp2zH9o&t=66s

Mercy https://www.youtube.com/watch?v=97DHnafJz6U

Dedicate House https://www.youtube.com/watch?v=9A66HDQGfLI&t=1686s

Heal My Foundation https://www.youtube.com/watch?v=UkJs7HnJfNk&t=12s

www.ingramcontent.com/pod-product-compliance
Lightning Source LLC
Chambersburg PA
CBHW070459100426
42743CB00010B/1685